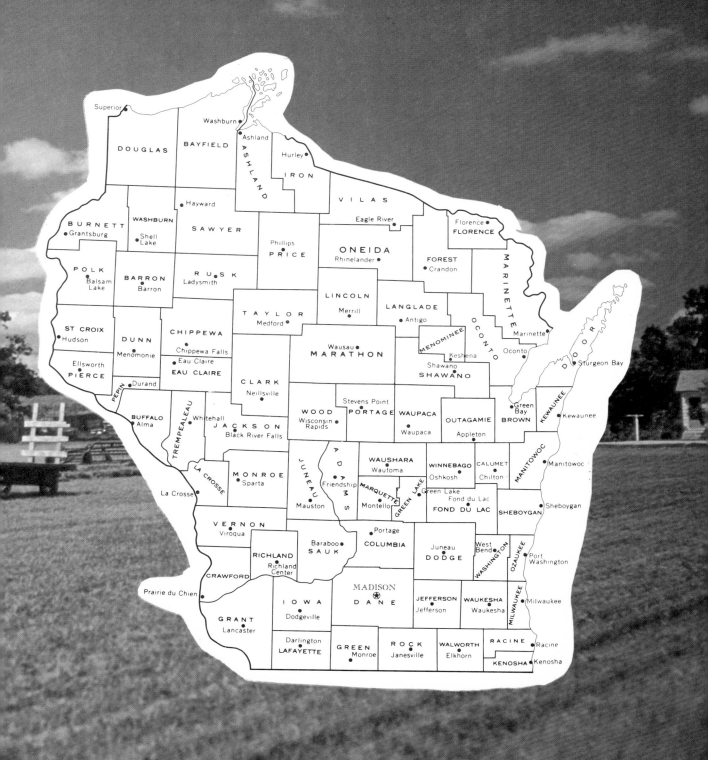

Enchantment of America
WISCONSIN

By Allan Carpenter

 CHILDRENS PRESS, CHICAGO

ACKNOWLEDGMENTS

For advice and assistance in the preparation of the revised edition, the author wishes to thank:
EARL J. GUSTAFSON, Public Information Officer, Department of Business Development,
Division of Tourism

American Airlines— Anne Vitaliano, Director of Public Relations; *Capitol Historical Society*,
Washington, D. C.; *Newberry Library,* Chicago, Dr. Lawrence Towner, Director; *Northwestern University Library*, Evanston, Illinois; *United Airlines*— John P. Grember, Manager
of Special Promotions; Joseph P. Hopkins, Manager, News Bureau.

UNITED STATES GOVERNMENT AGENCIES: *Department of Agriculture*— Robert Hailstock, Jr.,
Photography Division, Office of Communication; Donald C. Schuhart, Information Division, Soil Conservation Service. *Army*— Doran Topolosky, Public Affairs Office, Chief of
Engineers, Corps of Engineers. *Department of Interior*— Louis Churchville, Director of
Communications; EROS Space Program— Phillis Wiepking, Community Affairs; Charles
Withington, Geologist; Mrs. Ruth Herbert, Information Specialist; Bureau of Reclamation; National Park Service— Fred Bell and the individual sites; Fish and Wildlife Service—
Bob Hines, Public Affairs Office. *Library of Congress*— Dr. Alan Fern, Director of the
Department of Research; Sara Wallace, Director of Publications; Dr. Walter W. Ristow,
Chief, Geography and Map Division; Herbert Sandborn, Exhibits Officer. *National
Archives*— Dr. James B. Rhoads, Archivist of the United States; Albert Meisel, Assistant
Archivist for Educational Programs; David Eggenberger, Publications Director; Bill Leary,
Still Picture Reference; James Moore, Audio-Visual Archives. *United States Postal Service*— Herb Harris, Stamps Division.

For advice, counsel, and gracious help in the first edition, the author thanks:
Consultant Doris H. Platt, State Historical Society of Wisconsin; Irene Newman, State
Supervisor, School Libraries; M.G. Toepel, Chief, Legislative Reference Library,
Madison; Marathon County Historical Society, Wausau; Wisconsin Conservation Department.

Cover photograph: Sailing on Lake
   Geneva, Wisconsin Department of
   Natural Resources, Division of
   Tourism
Pages 2-3: A Wisconsin farm, Wisconsin
   Department of Natural Resources,
   Division of Tourism
Page 3: (Map) USDI Geological Survey
Pages 4-5: Milwaukee area, EROS Space
   Photo, USDI Geological Survey, EROS
   Data Center

Project Editor, Revised Edition:
   Joan Downing
Assistant Editor, Revised Edition:
   Mary Reidy

Library of Congress
Cataloging in Publication Data

Carpenter, John Allan, 1917-
Wisconsin.

(Enchantment of America)
  SUMMARY: introduces the history,
resources, industries, people, and tourist
attractions of the Badger state.
  1. Wisconsin—Juvenile literature.
[1. Wisconsin] I. Title
F581.3.C3 1978 977.5 77.13666
ISBN 0-516-04-49-5

1 2 3 4 5 6 7 8 9 10 11 12 R 85 84 83 82 81 80 79 78

Contents

White-headed Eagle. Male.
FALCO LEUCOCEPHALUS.

The bald eagle, the same as Old Abe, was painted by John James Audubon. Because the eagle's head is covered with white feathers it gives the appearance of being bald. Many hunters and trappers killed the bald eagle, but now it is protected by Federal law in the United States.

A True Story to Set the Scene

OLD ABE FLIES AGAIN

Black smoke poured out of the building in a dense cloud. The Capitol of Wisconsin was on fire. Firemen who rushed to the burning building on that February day in 1881 heard terrible and pitiful screams coming from the basement. The rescuers pushed into the choking smoke clouds and shortly after, to the cheers of the spectators, came out again, tenderly caring for the rescued screamer.

The rescuers had with them not a person, but an enormous eagle. The story of how a bird came to be kept in the basement of the Wisconsin Capitol and of how that bird had gained its great fame is just one of the many stories of the enchantment of Wisconsin.

The story begins at maple-sugaring time just twenty years before the fire in the Capitol, when America was just beginning the Civil War. For a bushel of corn, a famous old-time fiddler, Dan McCann, had bought the young eagle from an Indian who had captured him in the Flambeau River country. McCann played army music to the bird on his violin, hoping to sell him to an army unit being formed to fight the Civil War.

At Eau Claire, boys of Company C of the Eighth Wisconsin Battery scraped together five dollars and bought the eagle.

Named Old Abe, in honor of Lincoln, the eagle soon became a favorite, and earned his boys the nickname "Eagle Regiment."

His friends in the regiment made him an impressive perch in the form of a shield painted red, white, and blue. In Madison during a parade Old Abe was so excited by his favorite marching music that he sprang off his perch, grabbed a corner of the U.S. flag in his beak, and helped to carry it throughout the parade.

When the Eagle Regiment paraded through Chicago on its way to the war front, the eagle proved to be a great attraction. The Chicago Tribune said he was called "Old Abe — A majestic bird and well trained . . . (his men) . . . swear it shall never be taken by the enemy. No doubt, the Eau Claire Eagles and their pet bird will be heard of again."

9

During a military parade in St. Louis, Old Abe broke loose from his perch in his excitement at the music and soared high into the air, screaming. The incident broke up the parade while the Eagle Regiment scattered to recapture their mascot.

One of his favorite activities was stealing chickens from the regimental cook, and the soldiers often enjoyed watching the cook muttering under his breath as he chased the eagle down the company streets. Old Abe was gentle with his keeper, but if anyone tried to tease him, he would remember the person from that time on, watching for his chance to get even by clawing and scratching him.

In his first real battle at Corinth, Mississippi, Old Abe tore loose and flew into the thick of the fighting, screaming his war cry of encouragement to his boys. Although he took part in forty-two battles, he was never wounded. He had countless narrow escapes, however, and lost many a feather as the bullets whizzed by.

After the war, Old Abe was returned to Wisconsin and presented to the state. An offer to buy him for $20,000 was made by the famous circus man, P. T. Barnum, but the offer was refused. Income from his photographs, pamphlets describing his war experiences, and feathers from his wings and tail added considerable amounts to war charities. His feathers were sold for as much as $400 apiece.

Abe made his home in a large cage in the Capitol basement at Madison, but he had triumphal appearances everywhere. He was a star of the veterans' meeting at Chicago in 1875, and made a great hit at the World's Fair at Philadelphia in 1876.

After the fire in the Capitol, Old Abe lived on for a time, but he never fully recovered from the effects of the smoke and died on March 28, 1881.

Even after death, Old Abe continued to be an attraction. He was mounted and kept on display in the Capitol museum, until the museum was destroyed by fire, and along with it the remains of the famous eagle.

Today, a marker near the spot where he is supposed to have been captured as a young bird commemorates Old Abe's war service, and another stuffed eagle is still kept in the Capitol Building in his memory.

Lay of the Land

The name Wisconsin comes from an Indian word meaning "where the waters gather." This is an appropriate name since the waters of more than 10,000 streams and 8,700 lakes gather within the boundaries of the state.

Long before there were man-made highways, the rivers and lakes were serving as highways for Indians and early white settlers. These waterways have had an important place in the history of Wisconsin.

Among the important rivers are the Mississippi and the St. Croix — which form much of the western boundary of the state — the Wisconsin, Fox, Rock, Chippewa, Black, and Flambeau.

At one point the Fox River, which flows into Lake Michigan through Green Bay, and the Wisconsin River, which flows into the Mississippi, almost meet. If these rivers had met, men could have traveled by small boat from one side of the state to the other.

Where they come the closest, near Portage, these two rivers are only about 1½ miles (about 2.4 kilometers) apart. This meant that early travelers could cross Wisconsin by boat simply by carrying their canoes across the narrow stretch of land. This fact made the Wisconsin area one of the greatest gateways of the New World.

The mouth of the Wisconsin, painted by Henry Lewis.

Balance Rock in the Wisconsin Dells.

Largest of the inland lakes is Lake Winnebago, but it is small compared to lakes Superior and Michigan, to the north and east of Wisconsin.

The story is told that Wisconsin got its many inland lakes when the imaginary lumberman Paul Bunyan decided to jump into the Wisconsin River from the top of Rib Mountain, in the center of the state. The great splash scattered water all over the countryside, creating all the lakes.

At one time parts of Wisconsin were probably covered by shallow oceans, and these came and went several times, untold millions of years ago.

In later years, great glaciers of ice pushed down from Canada and covered much of what is now the northern United States. This happened four times, and part of Wisconsin was smothered with thick masses of ice during these "ice ages." Strangely, however, the ice divided into two parts as it is moved south and never covered the southwestern quarter of present-day Wisconsin, although it went around it and extended much farther south before it stopped. It would seem that sturdy old Rib Mountain had split the mass of ice apart and sent it around what is now called the "Driftless Area."

The glaciers ground over the rest of the state. They leveled the hills and filled in the valleys and when the ice finally melted, low places were filled in with water and became lakes. It is interesting to note that in the driftless area there are very few lakes, making it plain that Wisconsin owes its lakes to the glaciers.

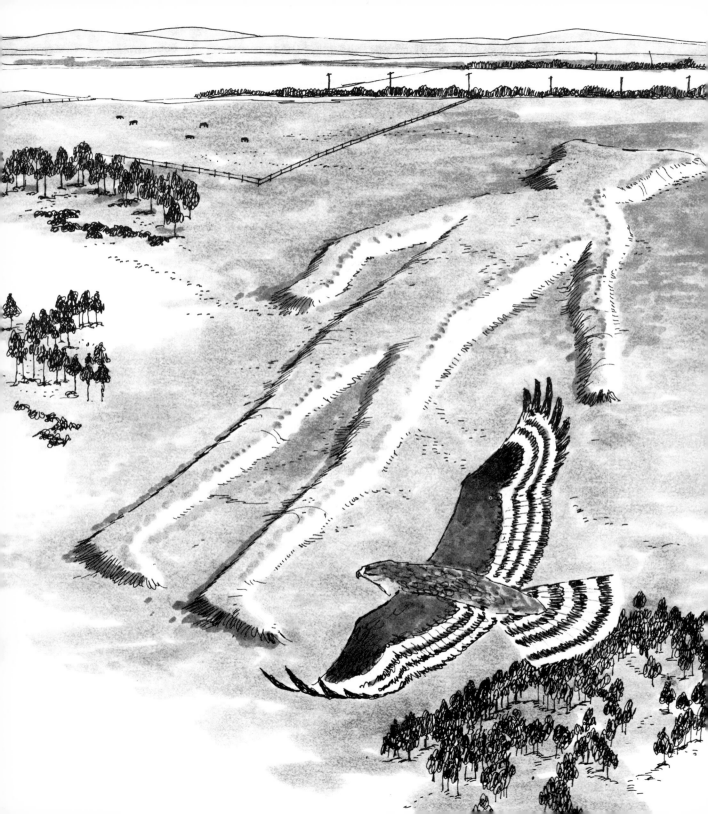

Footsteps on the Land

No one knows how long human beings have been in the land we call Wisconsin or who the first people may have been. Until the coming of the white man there were no written records of such things. However, even thousands of years after these people died, we are still discovering things that tell us something about them.

As long as eight thousand years ago, people now called Copper Culture Indians lived in Wisconsin. They knew how to pound copper and hammer it into useful items and jewelry. One of their burial grounds was found near Oconto on the north bank of the river.

Many early people piled up huge mounds of earth for various purposes. Some of the mounds merely looked like small hills, while others were formed in the shape of serpents, turtles, and other animal figures. These were called effigy mounds. Some of them were burial mounds, used as cemeteries, and others were not.

Near Baraboo is the famed "Man Mound," shaped like a man 150 feet (about 45 meters) tall and 50 feet (about 15 meters) broad at the shoulders. Other mounds can still be seen in parts of the state.

The most interesting reminder of forgotten people is a village ruin found near Lake Mills. It was described in 1836 by Judge N. F. Hyer. He thought it was the remains of an ancient city made by the Aztecs of Mexico because its pyramid-shaped mounds resembled those made by the Aztecs. So he named the area Aztalan.

At its peak Aztalan was a village surrounded by strong walls, some 19 feet (about 5.7 meters) high. The walls were of unusual construction, and nothing like them has been found in the state.

It now appears that the people who built Aztalan did have some connection with the Aztec from Mexico. They were entirely different from their Wisconsin neighbors. Some Aztec peoples had come up the Mississippi Valley, but the village at Aztalan is the farthest north that any traces of them have been found.

In many ways the people of Aztalan were more advanced than their neighbors. They made products of bone, shell, antler, stone, and sheet copper. But in one way they were no more civilized than the lowest savages. It is clear from the evidence they left that the people of Aztalan were cannibals. Some Indian tribes ate a portion of a human body as part of a ceremony, but the Aztalan people apparently hunted and ate other humans simply for food.

It is no wonder that their village was burned, probably by their neighbors, the Woodland Indians, in revenge.

It is likely that Aztalan was occupied for four to five hundred years. Strangely enough, it is thought that its cannibal people were there until less than a hundred years before the white man came.

THEY CAME WITH A BANG

One autumn day in 1634 all the men, women, and children of the Indian village at Red Banks near the head of Green Bay were standing on the shore gazing out over the waters of the bay. They had been told that a new kind of person would appear to them.

As they watched, a boat came down the bay carrying a pale-faced stranger. That stranger was dressed in a most wonderful costume — a robe of Chinese silk, beautifully embroidered, and a hat with fluttering plumes.

In each hand the stranger carried an odd-looking stick. When he reached the shore he raised his hands and thunder came out of each stick. To the frightened Indians he seemed like a god. The Indian chiefs all offered feasts in his honor, and everyone smoked the pipe of peace.

The man in the gorgeous robes was Jean Nicolet, the first white man known to have set foot on what is now Wisconsin. He had been sent by the French Governor of Canada to make friends with the Indians and possibly to find a passage across America to the rich shore of China.

Nicolet wore his expensive Oriental costume to impress Indians or Chinese officials, and when he came to the western shore of Lake Michigan, he thought he might be arriving in China. He must have been as surprised as the Indians were.

Jean Nicolet landed at Red Banks near Green Bay in 1634.
Here are two paintings depicting his landing.

The Indians who had greeted Nicolet were members of the Winnebago, a branch of the warlike Sioux group.

Many Algonquian Indians had come to the Wisconsin region because they had been driven farther west from their homes by the fierce Iroquois. By 1654 several Algonquian groups—Kickapoo, Mascouten, Potawatomi, Sauk, Chippewa, Fox, Huron, Ottawa, and Miami—had established villages in Wisconsin. Another Algonquian group, the Menominee (which means "wild rice eaters"), has been one of the most important Indian groups in Wisconsin ever since the members arrived there.

Menominees have always been outstanding people. They were noted for their friendship with the white man, and for keeping their word.

An unusual custom of the Menominee and some others was their wedding ceremony, which consisted of an exchange of blankets. If the marriage did not turn out to be satisfactory, the dissatisfied partner returned the blanket and the marriage was dissolved.

Chief Oshkosh, for whom the city of Oshkosh was named, was a prominent Menominee. Another Indian for whom a town was named was Queen Marinette. Today, many of the Menominees still live on lands where their forefathers lived in the days of the first white men.

FRANCE AGAINST ENGLAND

Twenty years passed since Nicolet's visit before another white man visited Wisconsin soil. This was Médart Chouart, Sieur de Groseilliers, accompanied by another Frenchman whose name we do not know.

On another trip, Groseilliers came with Pierre Esprit Radisson. Radisson wrote how tremendously impressed he was with the advantages of Wisconsin. "Grieve only that the rest of ye world could not discover such enticing countrys to live in."

Groseilliers and Radisson were the first French fur traders in the area.

18

The dress of high-ranking local chiefs combined Indian, French, and British influences. This might be Chief Oshkosh.

Along with the traders came French missionaries, devoted men who were determined to give the Indians an opportunity to learn about Christianity. One of the first "Black Robes" to labor in Wisconsin was Father René Ménard. He was an old man who suffered many hardships; he died when he became lost in the Wisconsin wilderness.

A few years after Father Ménard's death, in 1665, a second Jesuit missionary, Father Claude Allouez, took over the missionary duties of Father Ménard and established the Mission of St. Francis Xavier at Oconto.

Father Allouez was followed by Father Henri Nouvel. A trader, Nicolas Perrot, had brought Father Nouvel a beautiful silver monstrance for use in his chapel. When the chapel burned one day, one of Father Nouvel's Indian friends, Flying Bird, rescued the missionary's precious monstrance but later died of burns. Priests of Wisconsin made converts who were willing to sacrifice a great deal

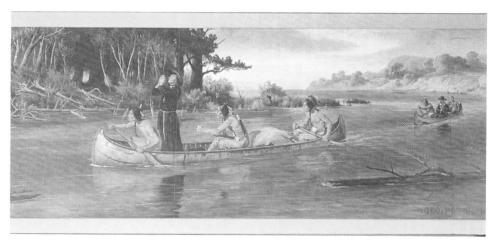

Marquette and Jolliet enter the Mississippi. Painting by George Peter.

for their newfound beliefs, even to giving up their lives as Flying Bird had done.

Just what happened to the monstrance after that is not known, but more than a hundred years after its rescue in the fire, in 1802, a Frenchman found it while digging a foundation for his home. Today the monstrance is a prized exhibit of the Neville Public Museum at Green Bay.

The best-known priest to travel and preach in Wisconsin during this early period was Father Jacques Marquette. In 1673 Father Marquette and the explorer Louis Jolliet set out from the Green Bay area on what has become one of the most famous of all exploring expeditions.

They took advantage of the wonderful water route up the Fox River and then crossed the narrow strip of land to the Wisconsin River, the route later used by traders. As far as we know, Marquette and Jolliet were the first white men to discover the upper Mississippi. They reached the Mississippi by following the course of the Wisconsin until it ended at the larger river.

When he saw that great river, Father Marquette wrote that he had "a joy that I cannot express." As they traveled down the "Father of Waters," Marquette told the Indians about Christianity, while Jolliet made notes about the land and people. They returned by way of Illinois and paddled up the west shore of Lake Michigan.

Father Marquette was loved by many of the Indians, and he continued his missionary work among them until his death only two years after his great exploration.

Because they were the first white people in the region, and because their traders and missionaries had done most of the exploration and settlement in the area, in 1671 the French claimed ownership of a great stretch of land in North America, which included what is now Wisconsin.

The English disputed that claim, and for almost seventy-five years conflict went on between England and France over who would control most of the continent.

There were few French settlers on the western lands. Other Frenchmen such as Duluth, Hennepin, and La Salle explored and traded, but most Frenchmen preferred staying at home rather than coming to the colonies.

Traders and missionaries had been in the Green Bay area for 111 years before the first permanent settlement in Wisconsin was begun at Green Bay in 1764. Another seventeen years passed before the second settlement was started in Wisconsin at Prairie du Chien in 1781. As late as 1800 there were only two hundred permanent settlers in all of Wisconsin.

When the British had finally driven the French government out of North America, Wisconsin became a part of the British territories in 1763. This arrangement was to last only a short time. The American colonies of Britain on the Atlantic Coast began the Revolutionary War which separated them from the mother country. In 1783 the British ceded to their former colonies lands which included Wisconsin. The war had little if any effect in Wisconsin.

Although the British had agreed to give up the Wisconsin area in the treaty of 1783, they refused to do so, and they were not completely dislodged until 1815, at the end of the War of 1812.

Wisconsin did not figure prominently in the War of 1812, but one event was the capture and burning of Fort McKay by the British. The fort had been built at Prairie du Chien by the Americans in 1813.

TERRITORIAL DAYS

Wisconsin is one of the six states that have come from what once was called the Northwest Territory. The Northwest Ordinance, the act that set up this territory in 1787, provided that its various regions would be governed by the Federal government until they were ready to become states. This ordinance was important because it gave other areas, in addition to the thirteen original colonies, a chance to become equal states rather than having to remain colonies of the central government.

Before Wisconsin became a state it was also a part of Indiana Territory, Illinois Territory, and Michigan Territory.

After the War of 1812, lead mining began to increase in southwestern Wisconsin. The mining towns of Wisconsin and Illinois were as rough and tough as those that grew up much later in the gold mining booms of California and Alaska.

Wisconsin was a western frontier. There were gunfights and gang brawls, and a social evening usually consisted of relaxing in the "lighthouses" — as the saloons were called — drinking "fusel oil" or "forty-rod," playing poker for a month's wages, or gathering to watch a horse race or a wolf fight.

Many miners refused to take time to build houses for themselves. Instead they burrowed into the sides of hills like badgers. Soon they came to be called "Badgers," and Wisconsin became the Badger State. The towns of Platteville, Shullsburg, and Mineral Point grew rapidly, and Mineral Point became the center of mining activity.

Almost as quickly as it had begun, the mining boom let up. The greatest part of the lead had been worked out.

By 1829, there were fifteen hundred people in the lead region, so a new county was formed with Mineral Point as the County Seat. The Federal judge, James D. Doty, held court there for the first time in 1830.

In 1832 settlers of Wisconsin and Illinois received a great fright. The noted Indian Chief Black Hawk brought his people back across the Mississippi from Iowa. The Indians had gone to Iowa when they signed a treaty giving up their lands in Illinois.

Prairie du Chien in 1830, painted by Henry Lewis.

Black Hawk said he was not on the warpath, but that he only
wanted to go north where he might find friends and land. But the
United States government called out troops to force him back across
the Mississippi, and the Black Hawk War began.

Slowly Black Hawk and his tribe were pushed northward along the
Mississippi River into Wisconsin. With food and ammunition almost
gone, Black Hawk tried to surrender, but the government forces
pushed on. He attempted to get his women and children back across
the Mississippi to safety in Iowa, but many of them were drowned or
shot as they were swimming the river. Black Hawk's warriors were

defeated. Of all the sixteen hundred Indians who came with Black Hawk originally, only a handful remained alive.

This was the last Indian uprising east of the Mississippi River. The Wisconsin town of Victory, near the scene of the last battle with Black Hawk, received its name from this victory.

Formed in 1836, the last territory to include Wisconsin before it became a state was given the name Wisconsin Territory. In addition to Wisconsin, the territory included Iowa, Minnesota, and part of the Dakotas. Belmont was named the capital.

Since Belmont was only a temporary choice, the territorial lawmakers had to choose a permanent capital. Everyone had his favorite among existing towns. No choice received enough votes. Finally Judge Doty suggested that the delegates choose a spot where no city yet existed and build a capital city from the beginning. Judge Doty owned a large amount of land in a beautiful lake region, and he persuaded the legislature to choose this location, which he had named Madison, in honor of the fourth President of the United States.

There were many complaints that Judge Doty had bribed the legislators to choose his location by giving many of them valuable lots in the unbuilt town. But no legal action was ever taken, and Madison has grown to be one of the most beautiful capital cities anywhere.

When the first Capitol building at Madison was almost completed, the legislature held a meeting there. Heating had not yet been installed. Ink froze in the inkwells on the legislators' desks. When heat finally came, the green boards that had been used opened up with cracks so wide the lawmakers could stick their hands through them. The basement of the building was being used as a pig sty, and the squeals of the porkers mingled with the arguments in the legislature above. Gradually improvements came to this first Capitol building at Madison.

In 1842 the Wisconsin territorial legislature was the scene of a murder. During the course of a quarrel between two of the legislators, Charles Arndt and James R. Vineyard, Arndt struck Vineyard in the face, knocking him backward. Vineyard drew a pistol and shot Arndt to death. Although Vineyard was tried over a year later, he was freed.

This painting by Henry Lewis shows the Battle of Bad Axe that ended the Black Hawk War in 1832.

The city of Milwaukee around 1872, painted by
A. C. Warren, who specialized in city views.

Milwaukee was incorporated in 1846 and the state as a whole had grown to the point where statehood was considered. In the short twelve-year period between 1836 and 1848, the population had skyrocketed from 22,000 to almost 250,000. In 1848, Congress approved the bill making Wisconsin the thirtieth state of the Union, with Nelson Dewey as its first governor.

Yesterday and Today

EVERYBODY FROM EVERYWHERE

By 1848 most of the Indian lands in Wisconsin had been signed over to the U.S. by treaty. The large tracts of inexpensive land available, and the prospect of having a vote, quickly attracted numbers of fine foreign settlers to Wisconsin. In Wisconsin, settlers from other countries who intended to become citizens were permitted to vote after living in the state for only one year.

Huge numbers of Germans came to Milwaukee and the southeastern area of the state until Wisconsin came to be thought of as a second Germany. The Germans brought many of their customs with them, including the Christmas tree and other Christmas customs that have spread over the rest of the country.

Many Scandinavians, Swiss, and even Icelanders, swarmed in to share in the advantages of the new state.

Internal improvements were planned or being built everywhere. The first railroad in Wisconsin, from Milwaukee to Waukesha, opened in 1851. People were so eager to have railroads that farmers mortgaged their land to help build them, and one locomotive was hauled to its tracks over a plank road. It took forty horses to do that job!

In 1853, Wisconsin passed a law outlawing the death sentence for criminals.

The next year a group of politicians met at Ripon because they were dissatisfied with the existing political parties. Meeting in an old school building, they formed the Republican Party on March 20, 1854. Ripon claims this makes it the birthplace of the national Republican Party, but two other states claim the honor, and the conflict has never been settled. In any event, the little schoolhouse where the convention was held has been preserved as an historic site.

The Republicans elected their first governor of Wisconsin, Coles Bashford, in 1856. However, the former governor, William Barstow, appeared to have been re-elected, and Barstow took the oath of office. Bashford was sworn in by the Chief Justice because both of them believed a recount of the votes would show that Bashford had won. When a recount was taken, Bashford was declared the winner, but Barstow held out in the governor's offices until Bashford forced him to leave.

Also in 1856, at Watertown, Mrs. Carl Schurz opened the first kindergarten to be operated in America. Mrs. Schurz was familiar with work that had been done in the kindergartens in Germany, and she felt the same thing should be done for the children of America.

Wisconsin took the first step toward its leadership as a cheese-making state when Hiram Smith made cheese in 1859, although large-scale commercial cheese making did not begin until Chester Hazen set up a cheese factory at Ladoga in 1864.

During the period when the state was growing rapidly in population and activity, its people were also growing more and more concerned about the great argument that was rapidly dividing the people of the United States. This was the question of whether people could be bought and sold and owned as slaves.

There were many abolitionists in Wisconsin who wanted to do away with slavery.

The experience of Joshua Glover in 1854 served to turn a large number of Wisconsin people against slavery. Glover was a black who had escaped from his master and was living in Racine. His master recaptured him and Federal marshalls took Glover to jail in Milwaukee.

Sherman M. Booth, the editor of an abolitionist paper, the *Daily Free Democrat,* rode through the streets of Milwaukee calling for people to assemble at the jail at two o'clock in the afternoon. Thousands answered this call. At six o'clock they rushed the jail, broke down the doors, and set Glover free. The people then paraded him through the streets of Milwaukee while he jubilantly sang "Glory, Hallelujah! Glory, Hallelujah!" Then he disappeared and was taken secretly to freedom in Canada.

Booth, who was considered responsible for setting Glover free, was sent to jail for causing a riot. He was freed by the state Supreme Court. Then followed a long struggle between the state courts, trying to keep Booth out of jail, and the United States courts, claiming that the state courts had no right to declare the United States courts to be wrong. Finally the United States arrested Booth, who promptly escaped. He was arrested again at Berlin, Wisconsin, and it appeared that he would have to finish his sentence, but he was pardoned by President Buchanan.

THE SOUTH AGAINST THE NORTH

When the Civil War came in 1861, Wisconsin was somewhat better prepared for it than some of the other states because of the foresight of Governor Alexander Randall. Wisconsin men volunteered so eagerly that the state was well ahead of its quota. Before the war was over, 91,379 troops from Wisconsin had seen service. And this was from a total state population of only 775,881.

In 1862 Louis P. Harvey, called the "seventy-three day governor," took office. He intended to be the solders' friend. When reports came of the heavy casualties among Wisconsin troops at the battle of Shiloh, the governor called on Wisconsin citizens to donate medical supplies, and he volunteered to deliver the supplies to the Wisconsin soldiers personally, which he did.

In a letter from Shiloh, the governor wrote, "Thank God for the impulse which brought me here. I am doing a good work and shall stay as long as I am profitably employed."

But his errand of mercy had a tragic ending. While trying to get from one steamboat to another, he fell into the Tennessee River. The swift currents carried him away, and his body was recovered nearly sixty miles downstream. Governor Harvey had been in office only seventy-three days. The soldiers of Wisconsin had lost a good friend.

However, the governor's wife, Cordelia Harvey, determined to carry on her husband's work in helping the servicemen. She knew that Wisconsin men were dying in Southern hospital camps because of the climate, so she decided to take this problem directly to President Lincoln.

The President was not at all pleased with this lady's interference.

But after she had seen him three times, the President finally issued an order establishing army hospitals in the cool and healthful climate of Wisconsin. By the war's end there were three such hospitals in the state. The one at Madison was named in honor of the late Governor Harvey. Mrs. Harvey came to be called the "Wisconsin Angel." After the war she was responsible for turning the Harvey hospital at Madison into a home for war orphans.

Among the many men of Wisconsin who won fame for their bravery during the Civil War were the three Cushing brothers. The youngest, William B. Cushing, had gained national fame for his heroism by the time he was twenty-one. He went from one daring accomplishment to another. One of these was the sinking of the

Wisconsin volunteers in the Battle of Williamsburg were typical of the men who represented their state in the Civil War. Color lithograph by Kurz and Allison.

Confederate ship *Albemarle,* which he torpedoed from a small boat. Only Cushing and one of his men ecaped alive. This episode helped to prove the value of torpedoes in naval warfare.

The two older brothers took part in many heroic actions. Alonzo B. Cushing was killed during Pickett's charge. The oldest brother, Howard B. Cushing, was called by his junior officer "the bravest man I ever saw."

Another Wisconsin man saved a whole Union fleet. In 1864 a force of gunboats started up the Red River to help in the Union attack on Shreveport, Louisiana. The attack was not altogether successful, and the Union forces, including the boats, were in danger behind the enemy lines. When the gunboats tried to turn back, they found the Red River had become so low that the fleet could no longer steam back to New Orleans.

Lieutenant Colonel Joseph Bailey, an engineer, had been a lumberman in Newport on the Wisconsin River, and he knew how to get lumber downriver in low water. He and his lumberjack crew built a dam — in only eight days, to the surprise of everyone — and raised the level of the water enough so that the Union fleet could float downstream. A portion of that dam can still be seen near Alexandria during periods of low water, a monument to a Wisconsin man's imagination and ability.

At the end of the war a Wisconsin regiment shared part of the honor of capturing Jefferson Davis, the President of the southern Confederacy. Davis, himself, had been associated with Wisconsin. As a young graduate of West Point, he had rafted logs past the rapids of the Dells to build Fort Winnebago. At Fort Crawford in Wisconsin he first met Zachary Taylor's daughter, whom he later married.

AFTER THE WAR

No wartime battles came to Wiconsin's borders, but in 1871 the state was the scene of one of the worst tragedies of another kind.

In the evening of October 8, 1971, the people of Peshtigo were worried over the threat of fire. The whole season had been very dry, and the heavily forested lands around Peshtigo needed rain desparately. Forest fires had been reported in many areas. Suddenly, without warning, the town of Peshtigo seemed to burst into flames with a roar like a huge explosion.

Most of those who were saved had managed to get into the river. One person who spent several hours in the water recalls, "I saw nothing but flames; houses, trees, and the air itself were on fire."

When the fire burned itself out early in the morning, eight hundred Peshtigo people had died within a few hours' time. Nearby areas had been burned, too, and altogether more than 1,200 Wisconsin people died in fires in the northeast that autumn.

One of the unusual things about this tragedy is that it happened at the same time as the great Chicago fire that is so much better known. Compounding tragedy even more, on the same day another very bad fire swept almost entirely across the state of Michigan, killing hundreds. Four times as many people died in the Peshtigo area as in Chicago, and yet very little attention was paid to the plight of the Wisconsin region. However, other Wisconsin towns collected supplies and money for relief, and the survivors were cared for.

Most people who think that the automobile is a twentieth-century development would be surprised to learn that in 1873 Dr. F. W. Carhart of Racine made a steam horseless carriage which he called the "Spark."

The people of Wisconsin became so excited about horseless carriages that in 1875 the state legislature offered a prize of $10,000 to the person who could build a horseless carriage that would run 200 miles (about 321 kilometers), run backward, and be guided down the road by its operator.

The committee in charge arranged to pick the winner by holding a race from Green Bay to Madison. When the day of the race came there were only two competitors — a car from Green Bay and a car from Oshkosh. The Green Bay car had an arrangement of gears that gave it several speeds, while the Oshkosh car had only one speed, forward. However, the Green Bay car was so complicated that it broke down and never made it to Madison, while the Oshkosh car steamed home a winner at an average speed of 6 miles (about 9.6 kilometers) per hour. The judges gave $5,000 of the prize money for this accomplishment.

This is claimed to be the first race ever run between two automobiles. It took place in 1878.

During this same period a Wisconsin man invented a device that was almost as important as the automobile in changing the way people lived. This was the typewriter, invented in 1869 by C. Latham Sholes.

Still another important field pioneered by Wisconsin was that of electric power, which has probably changed the lives of as many people as the automobile and the typewriter.

The world's first plant to produce electricity from water power was located at Appleton. Some claim that this was the first public power generator of any type. The first alternating current service began at Madison in 1888.

In 1889, a former governor of Wisconsin, Jeremiah Rusk, became the first man appointed as Secretary of Agriculture of the United States, though he was not the first man to hold the office.

A PROGRESSIVE STATE

The turn of the century brought many changes to Wisconsin. In fact, the history of Wisconsin during this period is probably more unusual than that of any other state.

In 1901 the first native-born Wisconsin man became governor. This was Robert M. La Follette. Governor La Follette felt that government was not paying enough attention to the interests of the common people. He urged that laws be made to protect them from powerful groups that looked after only their own interests.

To put his ideas across, La Follette knew that he would have to take away the power of party bosses, who could do almost as they pleased about selecting candidates for office. In developing his progressive policies La Follette worked closely with interested University of Wisconsin professors, and in 1904 Wisconsin passed the first statewide primary election law. This meant that the people of Wisconsin had an opportunity to select the candidates their party would nominate for public office.

This law marked the beginning of La Follette's leadership in what came to be called the Progressive Republican Party.

Under the leadership of its governor, Wisconsin first passed social legislation that later was adopted by other states generally and by the United States Government.

Pensions for the blind were established in 1907, aid to dependent children in 1913, old age assistance in 1925, and unemployment compensation in 1932. This Progressive program has been called The Wisconsin Idea.

Other Progressive legislation included child labor laws, com-

Robert M.
La Follette

pulsory vocational education for employed children, a minimum wage law for women and children, an apprenticeship law, and a civil service act.

Changes were not confined to the state government. In 1910 Eau Claire became the first city to adopt the commission form of government.

WARS AND RUMORS OF WARS

When it appeared that the United States would be brought into World War I, Robert M. La Follette, who was then the senior United States Senator from Wisconsin, was strongly opposed to the U.S.

Traffic at Milwaukee's port increased when the St. Lawrence Seaway opened.

taking part in the war. He voted against measures for war preparation, against the draft, and against a joint resolution that a state of war existed with Germany.

However, when war did come, Senator La Follette supported the war effort, although he never changed his opinion that the country should not have become involved in the war. Because of his sincerity and courage, he weathered the criticism against his position and was re-elected to the Senate.

When the U.S. entered the war against Germany, many people were fearful of the attitude that might be taken by the very large German population in Wisconsin. Would these people of German background be in sympathy with the mother country? These fears proved generally to be false.

Almost 125,000 men and women from Wisconsin were in the armed services during the war.

During World War II, the state more than kept pace with its neighbors, making sacrifices and working long and hard to bring about the end of the war. Men and women from Wisconsin in the armed services totaled 350,000 in this war.

One hundred and thirty-two thousand men and women from Wisconsin were in service during the Korean war.

Since the time the Congressional Medal of Honor was established during the Civil War, thirty-four men who entered service from Wisconsin have received this highest honor.

UP-TO-DATE

In 1953 another kind of war—the baseball wars—came to Wisconsin. When the Braves moved to Milwaukee, the whole town became baseball mad. Enthusiasm reached its peak when the Braves won the 1957 National League pennant and went on to the World Championship over the New York Yankees.

In 1959 an event occurred for which Wisconsin had been waiting a long time. That was the opening of the St. Lawrence Seaway. This waterway opened the state's ports to most ships of all the oceans of

A modern re-creation of an Indian ceremonial dance.

the world. New opportunities for commerce now were possible, and the state was not slow to begin taking advantage of them.

In celebration of the seaway opening, Queen Elizabeth II and Prince Philip of Britain visited many of the cities on the newly enlarged waterway, and they stopped at Milwaukee on July 7, 1959. This was the first visit of reigning monarchs in the history of the city.

As part of the celebration, a task force of forty-seven naval vessels visited various Wisconsin ports. This was the first time in the history of the Great Lakes that such ocean-going vessels from the fleets had been able to come to those waters.

Another unique event occurred in Wisconsin in 1961. The U.S. Government gave up all claim to the Menominee Indian Reservation, and Menominee became the seventy-second county in the state. The properties of the Menominees became a corporation, with the people holding shares.

Immense forests on their lands made the Menominees one of the most completely independent groups in the country. The Indians were far wiser than the white men in their use of the forests. When the white man's wonderful trees had been cut away and only acres of stumps or blackened ground remained on their land, the Menominees were still harvesting the wealth of their trees, due to their good management, as they continue to do today. The Menominees are noted for being among the most successful of all Indians.

In the 1920s the Menominees successfully opposed the transformation of their reservation into a National Park.

On New Year's Day, 1975, the calm of Indian relations was broken dramatically when Roman Catholic property at Gresham was occupied by a group of forty-five Menominees. Because the property was not being used, and the owners, Alexian Brothers, apparently had no plans for use of the land in the near future, the Indians demanded that the property be turned over to them for hospital purposes.

For thirty-five days the Menominees occupied the property. Eventually they left voluntarily after reaching an agreement with the Alexian Brothers to turn over the land to the Indian peoples for a dollar and other considerations.

Above: Because early miners burrowed into the sides of hills like badgers, Wisconsin is called the Badger State. Below: A wild turkey.

Natural Treasures of Wisconsin

Although Wisconsin is not the richest state in minerals, there have been and still are many valuable deposits beneath the earth.

Rich veins of iron ore have been worked in the Lake Superior area. Most of the lead in the southwestern area has already been removed, but considerable zinc remains. Building stone, sand, and gravel all add to the mineral wealth of the state.

However, growing things have been the most spectacular natural resources of Wisconsin.

Almost the whole of the state was covered with forests of various trees of unbelievable value. The most sought after was the beautiful, tall, straight white pine, which provided knot-free boards of the greatest possible length and width. Wisconsin still boasts that the MacArthur pine at Newald is the world's largest eastern white pine tree.

Many other valuable evergreen and hardwood trees grew in abundance.

Almost every kind of wildlife found in the northern forests was plentiful in Wisconsin. The fur of the beaver was so valuable in fur-trading days that its pelt was used for money.

So many of the beautiful passenger pigeons took part in their annual migrations that flocks of the birds blocked out the sun, sometimes for hours. They are reported to have zoomed along at speeds up to 60 miles (about 96.5 kilometers) per hour.

Single flocks of passenger pigeons, it was estimated, might contain the unbelievable number of more than two million birds. When they settled to feed, the beating of their wings caused a strong wind.

In the spring of 1871 Wisconsin had the largest nesting of passenger pigeons ever recorded. In 1882, the same area had another large nesting, but that was the last good-sized nesting of the passenger pigeon ever seen. The birds quickly died out, and have been extinct for many years.

There is a good deal of discussion about whether the passenger pigeon might have been saved had it been protected from killing by commercial hunters. Millions were killed daily for food and sport during the nesting, but many experts feel that even without the slaughter the passenger pigeon could not have survived civilization and loss of so many of its nesting places.

Now Wisconsin carefully protects its wildlife, so many other kinds of birds and animals have been more fortunate than the passenger pigeon.

The whistling swan was very close to extinction, but these huge birds are making a comeback. In their northward migration, whistling swans make a stop each spring on Green Bay. Each year, residents of the Green Bay area can look forward confidently to seeing these wonderful swans sometime between the nineteenth and twenty-third of March. They never fail. Almost every whistling swan in existence makes the stop at Green Bay.

Wisconsin's huge game farm at Poynette is the largest of its kind in the world.

The People Use Their Treasures

HOW NOW, BROWN COW?

When the name Wisconsin is mentioned, many people think first of dairying. However, dairying was not important in the early days of the state. For many years the principal farm activity was wheat growing, and Wisconsin was the second largest producer of wheat. Then wheat diseases and the land's loss of fertility brought hard times to the wheat farmers.

More and more farmers turned to the raising of dairy cattle and the sale of milk and milk products. State experts developed new methods of improving cattle, increasing the amount of milk they could produce, and new ways of testing and using milk products.

As a result of this careful and scientific development, in 1919 Wisconsin took the lead in milk and milk products and has been the first-ranking dairy state ever since. Wisconsin produces 16 percent of

Farming is an important industry in Wisconsin.

Wisconsin's cheese is famous throughout the nation.

all the nation's milk. It ranks first in condensed milk, whole milk, evaporated, powdered, and malted milk, and second in butter.

There are almost two million milk cows in Wisconsin.

Wisconsin also ranks first in cheese. In a few cheese-making plants the old-fashioned processes have changed very little over the years, but the larger part of the output is now made in the most modern factories. Steam-heated stainless steel vats are filled with milk; rennet, from the membrane of a calf's stomach, is added. This is necessary to start the formation of the cheese. When the curds have formed, they are kneaded into the proper shape and plunged into tanks of icy brine, which is the first step in curing.

Some cheeses must be cured in racks in cold storage for seven or eight months. One writer described the scene in one of these curing rooms, "Through one chill loft after another I roamed where the great cheeses hung like golden lanterns or lay in the racks. Down the silent rows passed a cheese scraper, his sole function all the frigid day to trim the faint blue-green mold from aromatic wheels and globes and cylinders and bricks of cheese."

Children everywhere have a Wisconsin man to thank for one of their favorite milk products. Inventor William Horlick combined two of his state's principal products, malt and milk, and invented malted milk. The Horlick plant at Racine still puts these two tasty products together in one of the largest manufacturing operations of its kind.

FROM WILD RICE TO TAME CROPS

Probably the first crop to be harvested in Wisconsin was wild rice. Today wild rice is still being harvested by Indians with the same methods used by their ancestors.

Now, however, many other crops are grown—in fact, agriculture is a billion dollar a year industry in Wisconsin!

The state leads all others in green peas. It is also first in hay and alfalfa, second in beets, cabbage, sour cherries, and cucumbers for canning. The Martin orchard at Sturgeon Bay is the world's largest red cherry orchard. Corn, oats, tobacco, potatoes, snap beans, and onions are other important crops.

The cranberry marshes, centered at Wisconsin Rapids, produce the largest inland cranberry crop in the United States, and Wisconsin ranks second in total cranberry production.

The first contour farming in the United States was tried near Coon Valley. Farmers all over the world have imitated this method of plowing because it is the best for keeping the soil from washing off plowed fields.

Every August a muskie bake is held at Boulder Junction. Guides donate the fish which are served to vacationers.

Indians gathering wild rice.

The number of farms dropped from 130,000 in 1960 to 106,000 in 1970; as the number of farms grew smaller, the size of individual farms increased. Farm lands occupy about one third of Wisconsin's area.

FUR FARMS

Another kind of "farm" is important in Wisconsin. The state is the leader in producing mink pelts. Most of these are not trapped, as in the early days, but are carefully and scientifically raised on mink farms or ranches. Fifteen hundred mink farms in Wisconsin produce more than a million pelts a year. Of course, some mink are still trapped in the wild.

Before mink was as popular as it is today, Wisconsin led the country in production of fox pelts.

This lumber is used for making paper.

The days when fur trapping was the most important activity have long since gone, but modern-day trappers still do a relatively small, but steady, business in fur-bearing animals.

THE TALLEST PLANTS

After the fur business became less important, the next source of wealth in Wisconsin was lumbering.

Led by the beloved but imaginary Paul Bunyan, the lumbering industry provided a colorful, rough and tough period in Wisconsin history. As soon as the ice melted on the rivers in spring, the lumber drives began. Timber that had been cut previously was floated downstream in tremendous masses; the hard working lumberjacks, who mastered the speeding logs, broke up jams that occurred when logs piled up together.

"The worst jam I remember," one lumberman recalls, "was in 1882 when 70,000,000 feet (about 21,300 kilometers) of logs were jammed at Grandfather Falls. I worked on that jam two months . . . had as high as 150 men working on it at one time. We used cant hooks, pike poles and peaveys, and horses were hitched to ropes to pull piles of logs out into deep water."

If the "key" log in a jam was pulled loose, the whole jam would let go, often catching a lumberjack and drowning him.

At the many sawmills logs were cut into lumber. Sometimes the lumber was tied together into rafts to be floated downstream to market.

A Wisconsin woman has some interesting memories of those lumber rafts. "On one side of the dam there was a chute, where the water would rush down to the river below the dam . . . The raft would be pushed to the chute, the gates would be opened and down it would slide through the chute of water, to the river below.

"Once in a while we would be allowed to ride on the rafts, too. Of course, we couldn't go alone. Even Mama liked to go, and so we would pack a basket for lunch and supper and all climb up on the raft. We each stood beside a stack of shingles as we waited for the gates to open. There would be a rush of water and the raft would go down the chute at a slant. Then as it reached the river, it would nose under the surface of the water. That's when you had to be quick and hop up onto your bundle of shingles or you'd get all wet.

"Below the dam, the water didn't rush along, so we would float gently on our high raft, watching the fields go by. We would float all day. We had our lunch up there, using a bundle of shingles for a table. When it began to get dark, all the passengers would get off on the riverbank. Someone would be there to take us home."

Wisconsin still has much wooded area.

When their trees were gone, many communities became ghost towns. Others, such as Eau Claire, Hayward, Fond du Lac, and Black River Falls had to change their activities after the lumber boom.

There are still 16,000,000 acres (about 6,475,000 hectares) of wooded area in Wisconsin; some of it is still used for lumbering, but more for wood pulp. Thanks to careful planning and replanting, more wood is grown each year in Wisconsin than is being cut.

To find out more about the growth and quality of wood and to discover new and better uses for it, the government operates the U.S. Forest Products Laboratory at Madison.

Pulp wood is used in paper making, an extremely important industry that grew up in Wisconsin after lumbering declined. Wisconsin leads the nation in paper making. It is the state's third largest industry, and strangely enough it is ahead of dairying in its annual volume of business. Paper making in Wisconsin started in the Neenah-Menasha region. Now an almost unbelievable variety of paper products are produced in the state.

To help the paper industry produce better kinds of paper at lower cost, the Institute of Paper Chemistry is operated at Appleton.

Wisconsin's hardwoods are also valuable. At Laona, in Forest County, is the Connor Mill, world's largest hardwood sawmill. The largest hardwood-manufacturing operation in the United States is at Algoma.

FROM BENEATH THE GROUND

In many ways mining in Wisconsin went through the same stages as lumbering—from boom to bust. The lead-mining boom in the southwestern corner helped to bring in large numbers of new residents. In 1835 a group of miners came from Cornwall in England. They settled in Mineral Point and used the limestone they found in the area to build stone houses very much like those they had in the old country.

One of the earliest industries in the state was that of making lead shot for guns. The shot was usually made in what was called a shot tower. A group of Wisconsin miners built a shot tower on the Wisconsin River by sinking a long mine shaft straight down into a cliff. The bottom of the cliff was tunneled out to make an entry to the shaft. Shot was formed by forcing hot liquid lead through a screen to make drops of hot lead the size needed for the shot. This was done at the top of the tower. As the drops of lead dropped through the air in the shaft or tower, cooling and hardening as they fell, they became round and smooth. They splashed into a cold water pool at the bottom of the shaft and soon were ready to be shipped to buyers.

The finished shot, smelted lead, and even the lead ore itself were sent down the rivers on flatboats, or sometimes were taken on the lonely, rutted, 150-mile (about 241 kilometers) road overland to Milwaukee.

The lead boom lasted for only about thirty years; by 1850 most of the lead was gone. Many of the miners took up farming. Some went west to another mining boom—the gold rush in California.

In the northern part of Wisconsin another mine boom began, this time in iron. The boom centered around Hurley, and a railroad was built from Hurley to Ashland. From there the ore could be shipped out in Great Lakes boats to mills farther east. When the ore gave out, this mining region became a ghost area.

Today zinc is still mined successfully in Wisconsin, but the state does not receive much wealth from mining, although the world's deepest iron mine is found at Montreal in Iron County.

Building stone, sand, gravel, and other minerals are important, however. Wausau is the center for red granite cutting, and this stone is much sought after for its value in building. In fact, Wausau lies at the foot of a solid mountain of granite, Rib Mountain, 1940 feet (about 590 meters) high.

INDUSTRIOUS WISCONSIN

Milling was the first important industry in Wisconsin. Almost every village with water power available had a mill to grind the grain for the surrounding market. After the Civil War, because of the large amount of wheat then grown in the state, Wisconsin became one of the leading flour-producing areas, under the leadership of Milwaukee.

That city ranked among the leading flour-producing cities of the world and was the world's greatest primary shipping point for wheat. Neenah and Menasha also were prominent flour-milling centers.

Flour milling declined with the drop in Wisconsin's wheat production, but lumber milling grew in importance and helped to offset the loss of income from milling. In 1910 lumbering and its related activities formed the largest industry of the state. In ten years it dropped to seventh place.

As described earlier, the paper-making industry has generally replaced lumber milling. Paper making is responsible for other industries in Wisconsin, as well. A Beloit company produces more than half of all the paper-making machinery made in this country. One of these machines was longer than a football field and weighed five mil-

The transportation of milk is vital to the dairy industry.

lion pounds (about 2,260 metric tons). It could turn out a strip of newsprint paper a mile (about 1.6 kilometers) long in just over two minutes.

Much heavy machinery of other kinds is produced in the state. Seventy-seven of the one hundred and one steam shovels used in constructing the Panama Canal came from Wisconsin. Some of the most enormous of the present-day digging machinery is made in the state.

Wisconsin ranks first in the production of internal-combustion engines and industrial controls. The "rivers of beer" which flows from Milwaukee make it the nation's brewing capital, but the manufacturing of equipment for generating, transmitting, and distributing electric power is the city's leading industry. Milwaukee

Tractors are manufactured in Milwaukee.

leads the world in diesel and gasoline engines, outboard motors, motorcycles, tractors, wheelbarrows, and padlocks, as well as beer.

Some of the first aluminum utensils ever made were produced in Wisconsin, and the manufacturing of these has grown into a nationally known industry, concentrated in Two Rivers, Manitowoc, and West Bend.

Wisconsin now ranks third among all the states in the automotive industry.

Wisconsin producers of enamelware, such as bathtubs, give the state a ranking among the top three in these important products. The Kohler Plant at Kohler and the Vollrath Company at Sheboygan are leaders in this field.

In addition to dairy products, the processing of other foods is important. Commercial canning in the state began in 1887 when Albert Landretch set up his cannery at Manitowoc. Today, 40 percent of all the peas canned in the United States are processed in Wisconsin. Wisconsin canneries produce 20 percent of all the canned vegetables put up in the country as a whole.

KEEPING IN TOUCH

From the beginning, Wisconsin has been favorably situated for transportation and communication.

When the St. Lawrence Seaway opened, the first large ocean vessel to visit Milwaukee was the *Prins Johan Willem Friso* of the Niagara Line, flying the Dutch flag. The port of Milwaukee is said to be one of the most efficient in the world due to its large modern loading and unloading equipment. One ship captain who expected to take three days to unload his vessel at Milwaukee found the job done in only six hours.

Chequamegon Bay and Superior are generally regarded as having the finest harbors on the Great Lakes.

At Superior is the world's largest grain elevator.

Not all travel in Wisconsin is for the purpose of commerce. The sparkling lakes and thousands of fishing streams as well as the beauty and charm of the countryside and towns all make Wisconsin one of the leading tourist states. The tourist industry is well organized in Wisconsin, and there are fine accommodations almost everywhere.

Millions of tourists visit the state each year. Today the estimated annual income brought to Wisconsin by tourists alone exceeds three billion dollars.

Human Treasures

EARLY MEN OF FAME

"Father of Wisconsin" is the name given to a famous French settler, Charles de Langlade. Langlade went to war at the age of ten and claimed to have fought in ninety-nine different battles. In his old age Charles de Langlade wished that he might have been able to fight one more battle — in order to make his record an even hundred!

In 1764 Charles de Langlade settled at Green Bay, making the first permanent settlement in Wisconsin. He worked with John Jacob Astor and his American Fur Company.

Although most early Indian chiefs gained their fame as warriors, Tomah, chief of the Menominees and one of Wisconsin's outstanding chiefs, was best known as a man of peace. The great Indian warrior Tecumseh once sent a messenger to Tomah asking for his help in battle. The messenger made a speech to the Menominees about the glories of war and of his leader, Tecumseh.

Then Tomah spoke. He reminded his people of what the messenger had said about the number of scalps Tecumseh had taken, about how the blood flowed, and about the number of enemies who had been killed. Then Tomah lifted up his hands and told his people quietly but firmly, "It is my boast that these hands are unstained with human blood."

The Menominees did not go to war with Tecumseh.

Another chief of the Menominees, Chief Machickanee, was known for his unusual costumes. He enjoyed wearing a formal Prince Albert coat and high hat on ceremonial occasions, but he usually preferred to wear these formal clothes without his trousers at these ceremonies.

Still another early Wisconsin man who had his own manner of doing things was Justice of the Peace Pat Kelly of Hickory. When he was called upon to perform a wedding, it was sometimes impossible to find a witness, because of the small number of settlers in the region. Many of Justice Kelly's weddings were performed without human assistance — he swore in the nearest trees as witnesses!

French traders negotiating with the Indians.

Many of Justice Kelly's "Witness Trees" are still pointed out where they have been growing ever since.

Eleazar Williams was an early Wisconsin man of unusual history. He claimed to have no memory of his early boyhood. His first memories were of an Indian family in New York who adopted him. He grew up with them and became a respected missionary to the Indians.

After he came to Green Bay, Williams happened to meet the Prince de Joinville, who was traveling in the region. The Prince, who was the son of the French king, Louis Philippe, said that Williams was the lost Dauphin of France; at least this was what Williams claimed. The lost Dauphin was son of the King and Queen of France who were beheaded in the French Revolution. The Dauphin disappeared as a young boy, and his fate was never known. From that time on, Williams claimed to be the lost Dauphin, heir to the throne of France. He had little success in making people believe his story, however.

56

VERY CLEVER, THESE BADGERS

One of the reasons for Wisconsin's leadership in industry is the ability of her people to create new machines and methods for getting things done, or for saving lives, time, or money.

John Stevens invented the rolling mill process for milling flour in 1874.

In 1869, a Wisconsin man introduced one of the world's most important inventions. Christopher Latham Sholes made twenty-five different machines, and spent six years perfecting his idea, with the help of Carlos Glidden. His invention was the first typewriter.

At first, people were not very much impressed with the machine, but the famous writer Mark Twain bought and used one of the new "literary pianos" and praised it highly. At the centennial world's fair in Philadelphia in 1876, the typewriter caused a sensation. People paid twenty-five cents for a small piece of paper with typewriting on it. The business world hasn't been the same since.

One of Wisconsin's famous scientists was Increase Allen Lapham, who has been called the father of the United States Weather Bureau.

Lapham was the Wisconsin state geologist. He was interested in many scientific fields: he studied Indian mounds and collected rocks, plants, and shells. He realized how helpful it would be if people could be warned in advance about bad weather. Farmers might protect their crops from approaching storms; seamen might save their lives by putting into port when storms were expected.

In 1869 Lapham was able to persuade a Congressman from Wisconsin, H. E. Paine, to introduce a bill to establish a United States Weather Bureau. The Bureau was first set up in Chicago, with Lapham as its assistant director.

The first weather forecast sent from the signal tower in Chicago on November 8, 1870, proved to be exactly right, and the Weather Bureau has served the people of the country from that time on. In fact, some people have jokingly said that the Weather Bureau has been trying to live up to that first forecast ever since.

Another Wisconsin inventor was John Appleby. As a young man he knew how hard it was to gather and bind grain by hand in the

Evinrude outboard
motors are made
in Wisconsin.

fields. Because farm help was scarce, much wheat was being wasted. Appleby was sure that there must be a way to make a machine that would tie a knot in a bundle of grain. It took him nineteen years, but John Appleby finally invented a knotting machine to be attached to a reaper so that bound bundles of grain could be turned out as the reaper went through the field.

All boaters and fishermen should have a warm spot in their hearts for the Wisconsin man who invented and promoted the outboard motor, which has become so popular today. He was Ole Evinrude, and one of the popular outboards still made in Wisconsin bears his name.

Two men of science were especially important to Wisconsin's dairy industry. They were William D. Hoard and Stephen Babcock.

William Hoard has been called the father of modern dairying. He spent his life trying to improve dairying in his state. He encouraged farmers everywhere to improve their herds through breeding, better sanitation, and better feeding. He founded the Wisconsin State Dairyman's Association in 1872.

In the early days of dairying there was no way to determine the richness of the milk a cow was producing or evaluate the quality of the milk a farmer sold. Some farmers even put water in the milk to have more to sell.

Dr. Stephen M. Babcock set about finding a simple method of testing the richness, or butterfat content, of milk. He succeeded in 1890, and his process has been called one of the world's most important discoveries. Dr. Babcock's test was so simple that it could be used right at the farm or the dairy. He would not patent his test, so he probably gave up a large fortune by making his discovery available free to the world.

In the field of human health Dr. Babcock did research that may be even more important than his butterfat test. When he was on the staff of the Wisconsin Agricultural Station he conducted dairy feeding experiments that led to the discovery of vitamins.

Two other Wisconsin men have brought important institutions into being. William F. Vilas, as Postmaster General of the United States, recommended and began the important Rural Free Delivery of mail and the parcel post system. John Muir, who studied at the University of Wisconsin, is known as the father of our National Parks system.

FRIENDS OF THE MUSES

A famous figure in the field of sculpture was born at Madison. This was Vinnie Ream. She was the only sculptor Abraham Lincoln ever posed for. The President posed for five months—until the day before he was killed.

When Congress decided to have a figure of Lincoln modeled for the Capitol building, they chose Wisconsin's Vinnie Ream to do the work. She had won a competition entered by many other famous sculptors. This was the first time Congress had ever commissioned a woman for a work of sculpture. Congress paid her $15,000 for her work.

Annunciation Greek Orthodox Church designed by Frank Lloyd Wright.

Also in Washington is Vinnie Ream's bronze statue of Admiral Farragut. Her sculpture "The West" can be seen in the Capitol at Madison, and the Wisconsin State Historical Society has her "Spirit of the Carnival" on display.

Some famous Wisconsin writers have been Hamlin Garland of West Salem, George W. Peck, author of *Peck's Bad Boy,* Ben Hecht, Edna Ferber, and Ray Stannard Baker. Another Wisconsin author, Zona Gale, received the Pulitzer Prize for her play *Miss Lulu Bett.* The poet Ella Wheeler Wilcox, who wrote "Poems of Passion" and "The Way of the World," is also listed among one hundred great Wisconsin people.

On that same list, as prepared by the Wisconsin Centennial Committee in 1948, are Carrie Jacobs Bond of Janesville, the famous song writer, who wrote such great favorites as "The End of a Perfect Day," and "I Love You Truly"; Charles K. Harris, who wrote the song "After the Ball Is Over"; and the pianist and composer Alexander Mc Fayden.

WRIGHT OR WRONG?

Few men who are not in politics have had both the extreme praise and severe criticism that came to Frank Lloyd Wright during his lifetime. Mr. Wright was not a politician but an architect. There are many who call Mr. Wright one of the greatest architects who ever lived, and there are others who feel that his work was frightful. Most people are not neutral about Mr. Wright and his work but take strong views one way or the other.

Wright used his impressive building at Spring Green, Wisconsin as both a home and school. Leading architectural students came from all over to study under Mr. Wright at his home, Taliesin.

One of the last buildings that Wright designed before his death is one of the most discussed structures anywhere. This is the Guggenheim Museum of Art in New York City. Visitors take an elevator to the top floor of the building and see the pictures by walking down a corkscrew ramp.

The Johnson Wax Research Tower, located in Racine, rises more than 153 feet (about 47 meters) into the air. It was designed by Frank Lloyd Wright and completed in 1950.

Mr. Wright always looked ahead to the future, and one of his last ideas was to build a mile-high skyscraper in Chicago. Many people think this impossible, but others look forward to the day when Wisconsin's Frank Lloyd Wright will be remembered as the inspiration for the world's first building to tower a mile into the sky.

ROBERT M. LA FOLLETTE

One of the best-known political figures of his time—Robert M. La Follette—was not only the first native-born Wisconsin governor, but also the first governor to graduate from the University of Wisconsin.

When it was time for him to enter the university, he was poor, but his family moved to Madison so Robert could go to school while his widowed mother maintained a student rooming house.

La Follette worked his way through the university by teaching a country school.

He was an effective speaker and many of his friends urged him to become an actor; because of his small stature, theatrical experts persuaded him to go into some other field.

During La Follette's period as governor, plans for the present Wisconsin Capitol were started. The primary election laws were passed. Civil Service and a legislative reference library also were started during his terms.

From the governor's chair, La Follette went on to spend almost twenty years in the United States Senate. One friend said of him, "There is not a farmer in the fields, not a worker at a forge, not a brakeman on a freight, not a sailor on the sea, not a woman at her tasks, not a child in school whom La Follette has not helped."

Today, in the national Capitol building at Washington visitors can view the statue of Robert M. La Follette in the Nation's Hall of Fame.

OTHER FAVORITE SONS AND DAUGHTERS

The noted cartoonist, Clare Briggs, gained national fame for his drawings, such as the series "When a Feller Needs a Friend." Blanche Cork, of Oconto, won her place in the public eye as the "World's Champion Bareback Rider." Famed Dr. William Beaumont was stationed at Fort Crawford near Prairie du Chien, and did much of his highly respected experimenting and writing on digestion while a Wisconsin resident.

Cy Young, a great baseball player

Denton (Cy) Young, who played from 1890 to 1911, now in baseball's Hall of Fame, holds the record for most games won by a pitcher—511. Richard Ira Bong, Wisconsin World War II flying ace, shot down forty Japanese planes. Another noted Wisconsin military man was Civil War hero, Edward S. Bragg, commander of the "Iron Brigade."

Nor should the earlier and less prominent pioneers of Wisconsin be overlooked. The state owes much to the resourceful Indians, adventurous Frenchmen, black-robed priests, British redcoats, lumber barons, and husky lumberjacks who led the way.

64

Teaching and Learning

An eloquent expression of the attitude toward education that has characterized the University of Wisconsin since its founding in 1848 may be read from a bronze plaque that is mounted on one of the university buildings on the Madison campus. The words were taken from an 1894 report of the board of regents:

"Whatever may be the limitations which trammel inquiry elsewhere, we believe that the great state University of Wisconsin should ever encourage that continual and fearless sifting and winnowing by which alone the truth can be found."

The University of Wisconsin at Madison today is ranked by the Association of Research Libraries as first among universities in the training of persons for doctor's degrees of all kinds.

It has risen to this greatness in only a little over a hundred years. The university and the state of Wisconsin grew up together, both having been started in 1848. In 1849 the university was established in rented quarters of the Madison Female Academy.

Today it is considered one of the outstanding universities of the world.

The discoveries at the university bring more wealth to the state each year than the entire cost of running the university, according to a former president of the university, Dr. Charles R. Van Hise. Much of this wealth is due to the generosity of a later day Wisconsin scientist, Dr. Harry Steenbock. In 1929 Dr. Steenbock was searching for a cure for rickets. In one experiment he fed some hogs feed that had been under the rays of a sun lamp, and found that these hogs grew much faster than those hogs that had not eaten this light-treated feed. This led to the discovery that ultraviolet radiation produces vitamin D in foods.

A breakfast-food company offered Dr. Steenbock $900,000 for his patent rights. He refused the offer and instead turned his rights over to a foundation for the support of more research. This was the Wisconsin Alumni Research Foundation, called WARF, now connected with the University of Wisconsin. WARF has been one of the most successful organizations in the history of science.

Right: Dining room at Taliesin. Students from all over the world came to study architecture under Frank Lloyd Wright here. Below: The Student Union at the University of Wisconsin at Madison.

Above: Education takes many forms, as in the Period House Youth Center. Left: The Science Building of Marquette University and Gesu Church in Milwaukee.

WARF has developed Dicumarol, a very helpful drug to prevent blood from clotting; warfarin, one of the most successful of rat poisons; a strain of penicillin that has been especially valuable; and nicotinic acid, a cure for pellagra. These and many other developments have enabled WARF to put more than thirty million dollars into other much-needed research projects.

Another Wisconsin college of high rank is Lawrence, at Appleton. The college was chartered in 1847, and paper-making Appleton grew up around it. A Boston merchant, Amos Lawrence, gave the money and land to establish the college. This institution is rated by many as one of the top ten United States liberal arts colleges.

Lately Lawrence College has become known as the "Cradle of University Presidents." Three of its recent presidents have left Lawrence to become heads of famous universities. Henry M. Wriston, eighth president of Lawrence, became president of Brown University. In 1953, Harvard, the nation's oldest and richest university, made Lawrence president, Nathan M. Pusey, president of Harvard. In 1962 Duke University selected as president Douglas M. Knight, then the head of Lawrence.

On the Lawrence campus is the Worcester Art Center and the music-drama center. This is the headquarters of one of the leading college music departments, the Conservatory of Music.

Beloit College at Beloit is another prominent Wisconsin educational institution. The town of Beloit was founded by a group of New Hampshire people who were determined to keep the advantages of a good education available even in their new frontier home. They founded a seminary almost as soon as they arrived in Wisconsin, and this became Beloit College.

Among Beloit's distinguished former students the college points with special pride to the explorer Roy Chapman Andrews and the famous nationally syndicated cartoonist J. N. Darling, who was widely known as "Ding."

A prominent private educational institution of the Milwaukee area is widely recognized Marquette University. Five other colleges are found in the Milwaukee region, and the University of Wisconsin maintains a branch there.

The library mall at the University of Wisconsin in Madison.

Although it is small in numbers of students, Ripon College at Ripon is well known outside the state.

Altogether there are thirty-nine institutions of higher learning in Wisconsin.

Left: Fans pack Lambeau Stadium to watch the Green Bay Packers play. Below: Sailing on Lake Geneva in southeastern Wisconsin.

Enchantment of Wisconsin

AROUND A BAY OF GREEN WATERS

The tourist who begins his tour of Wisconsin in the Green Bay area does just what the first explorers did. These early explorers began their acquaintance with the land we know as Wisconsin in the area of the bay of green waters.

The city of Green Bay is the oldest permanent settlement in the state, and the Tank cottage in that city is the oldest building still standing in Wisconsin.

History of an entirely different kind is preserved at the National Railroad Museum at Green Bay, where old-time railroad locomotives and other equipment are preserved for public display. Here passengers can ride a railroad coach of yesterday, pulled by a puffing old steam engine. Very large, once prominent, locomotives are kept on the museum grounds, and some of them still get up steam.

Green Bay has achieved unusual recognition in the field of sports. It is by far the smallest city in the country to serve as headquarters for a major league football team. The Green Bay Packers consistently rank with teams of the large cities, as demonstrated by their championsnip teams and victory in the first super bowl.

Not far from the city of Green Bay is one of Wisconsin's favorite vacation lands — Door County. Gateway to this peninsula is the city of Sturgeon Bay. It takes its name from the wonderful sturgeon fishing in the early days. So many sturgeon were caught that they were piled on the shore like cordwood. Ship building, from pleasure boats to car ferries, is a major industry in Sturgeon Bay.

South of Sturgeon Bay, La Salle County Park marks the location where the explorer La Salle and fourteen of his companions were rescued from starvation by friendly Indians.

Farther north, three hundred Potawatomi Indians were not so fortunate as La Salle. They were traveling by canoe to do battle with their enemies, the Winnebagos, who had a camp near the tip of the Door Peninsula. They planned to come ashore quietly and surprise the Winnebagos. Instead, their canoes were dashed against a bluff,

Both downhill and cross-country skiing can be found in Wisconsin, especially in the north where the snowfall is usually heavy.

and all the Potawatomi were killed. The place where they died has been known as Death's Door Strait ever since.

Across Death's Door Strait from the mainland is Washington Island. Around the island are said to lie some of the richest fishing grounds in all of the United States.

Washington Island is famous for having this country's largest settlement of people of Icelandic descent.

Other Door County attractions include Fish Creek, where a famous summer music and theater festival is held each year, and Egg Harbor. This town got its unusual name from a battle of eggs that a group of Green Bay men held as part of a lighthearted vacation excursion.

Tornado Memorial Park in Door County is dedicated to those who died in a fire at the same time as the great Peshtigo fire of 1871.

Across the Bay in Oconto visitors may see the first Christian Science Church ever built; it was constructed in 1886. Also in Oconto County is Cathedral Woods, a small tract of virgin timber near Townsend, one of the few such forests remaining.

Farther south, on the Fox River route of the pioneers across Wisconsin, is De Pere with its nearby Lost Dauphin State Park, made from the 19 acre (about 7.6 hectares) estate of Eleazar Williams, who claimed to be the lost prince of France. Also on the

72

Fox River route is Appleton, said to be the first city to generate electrical water power for a general power supply. A replica of the original historic power station is on display in the town.

The first house in the United States to be wired for electricity may be seen at Appleton. This mansion on the river bank was converted into a restaurant in later years.

Also at Appleton is the Dard Hunter Paper Museum, displaying methods of paper making from paper's invention, shortly after the time of Christ, to the present.

South and west is Ripon, where a group called the Phalanx tried one of the many ideas of community living which were so common at one time. All property was held in the name of the group; all members lived in one long house and ate at one long table.

One of the oddest things about the Phalanx was its financial success. In a few years it had grown so rich that all its members decided to disband and divide the profits.

To the east, the northernmost of the larger Wisconsin cities on Lake Michigan is Manitowoc, home of the company that is the world's largest manufacturer of aluminum ware.

South of Manitowoc is Sheboygan, and west of Sheboygan is the noted Wade House. This building was built by Sylvanus Wade in 1851. It cost only $300 and soon became one of the most popular stagecoach stops on the whole frontier. It was restored by the Kohler Foundation under the direction of Ruth and Marie Kohler. Today visitors may see this interesting example of inn and stagecoach life of the past.

Coast Guard station at Door County.

Dominating the east coast is Wisconsin's largest city. Much of Milwaukee has been reclaimed from river bottoms of wild rice marshes and tamarack swamps.

Marquette and Jolliet in 1673 are thought to be the first white men to visit the site of Milwaukee. They found that the Indians called the area Malm-a-waukee Sape, which means "Gathering Place by the River." From this the present name was derived. The city itself was founded by Solomon Juneau, who settled on the east side of the Milwaukee River. The community was not incorporated as a city until 1846.

The city of Milwaukee

Mitchell Park Horticultural Conservatory, Milwaukee.

From a historical standpoint, one of the most interesting areas of Milwaukee is the harbor. The first ship to put into Milwaukee's harbor was His Majesty's sloop *Felicity,* in 1779. In the harbor is a point of land that used to be an island, called Jones Island. After the Civil War, squatters began to settle on this island. The population of Jones Island at one time reach three thousand. For years the island had its own informal government and it was said that no Milwaukee policeman dared to venture onto the island. Law enforcement was left to the local authorities, led by a Polish fisherman, Jacob Muza.

Finally the city decided to buy the island, and in 1914 the development of the island's harbor facilities began. It was not until 1943 that the last of the squatters gave up his claims and the old Jones Island was no more.

Milwaukee is noted among American cities for its low crime rate and good civic government. Its Public Museum is the fifth largest in the United States.

A Milwaukee suburb, Waukesha, is noted for its fine spring water. It was this spring water that led to an event called the Waukesha Water War. Some promoters at the 1893 World's Fair in Chicago were trying to get the permission to pipe Waukesha's precious spring water 100 miles (about 160 kilometers) to the fair. The request was refused. Then one night citizens of Waukesha were told "The pipeliners are coming!"

Men of the town grabbed their guns or any weapons they could find and went to defend the spring. They even hauled their souvenir Civil War cannon from the park to help with the defense.

A train load of laborers came in from Chicago to lay the pipe but the people of Waukesha warned them that if they put one pickax in the ground they would be mobbed. Finally the frightened workmen went back to their train and left for Chicago.

The next day the courts prevented any further work on the project, and Waukesha's famous spring water is still serving the town and its visitors. Today the people of Chicago and almost anywhere else can buy bottled Waukesha water.

Farther down the lake shore is Racine, said to have the largest population of people of Danish ancestry in the United States. It is the home of the Johnson's Wax Company and of the Horlick plant, where malted milk was originated.

Almost at the southeast corner of the state is Kenosha, noted as international headquarters for the Society for the Preservation and Encouragement of Barber Shop Quartet Singing in America and for American Motors' large plant.

Also in the southeastern area are Burlington, Janesville, and Beloit. Burlington is hailed as the headquarters of the famous Liars' Club, which conducts an annual humorous contest to choose the greatest liar of the year.

Janesville was founded by Henry O. Janes, who must have some sort of a record for founding towns named Janesville. In addition to the one is Wisconsin he founded other Janesvilles in Minnesota and in Iowa.

Beloit was founded when almost all the people of the town of Colebrook, New Hampshire, moved to Wisconsin.

Nearby Lake Geneva has long been noted as an exclusive summer resort, mostly for wealthy Chicagoans. The Yerkes Observatory on Lake Geneva has made notable discoveries in astronomy and is a favorite tourist attraction.

Principal city in south-central Wisconsin and main attraction for visitors is the capital, Madison, often said to be the most beautiful state capital in the United States.

Madison was built on the narrow strip of land between two lakes, Mendota, and Monona, and named for the fourth President of the United States, James Madison. In the city today is the second highest Capitol dome in the country. Wisconsin has had five Capitol buildings. The first, located at Belmont, was built from prefabricated pieces shipped from Pittsburgh, Pennsylvania.

The second was in what is now Burlington, Iowa; the third, on the site of the present building, was started in 1837. When this became too small, the legislature passed a bill in 1857 to enlarge and improve the old building. When the legislators got back to Madison for the 1858 session, they found that a new Capitol was being built. The legislators were startled, but they let the building go on.

Finished in 1869, the building was again too small by 1882, so two wings were added. One of these collapsed during construction, killing four men.

On February 27, 1904, the Capitol, except for the north wing, was destroyed by fire. Plans for the new building called for an unusual structure in the form of a Greek cross, with four identical wings radiating out from the rotunda beneath the dome.

This building was finished in 1917 at a cost of $7,258,763.75. It contains thirty-six different types of marble and granite. There was no dedication of this magnificent building and no record that a cornerstone was laid. Several state office buildings in various parts of the state now serve as Capitol annexes to house some of the state departments.

Visitors to Madison find much of interest in the buildings and grounds of the state university, with its ideal location on the shores of Lake Mendota. The university's arboretum is also worth a visit; its lilac plantation and wildlife preserve are especially interesting.

An aerial view of the Capitol at Madison.

Another institution of interest in Madison is the museum of the State Historical Society of Wisconsin, which houses, among other items of interest, the most complete collection of guns in the country.

Radio Station WHA at Madison is the oldest continuously operating radio station in the world. When the station first went on the air it had tubes that were made by local craftsmen and placed in glass globes specially blown for them by Madison glassblowers.

WHA was the first educational radio station, and it broadcast the first music-appreciation program ever sent over the air.

Not far from Madison, in the foothills of Blue Mounds, is Little Norway, a village built as it would have been in old Norway. The Norway building of the World's Columbian Fair (Chicago, 1893), a fine example of ancient Norse church architecture, was moved to Little Norway. A fine collection of Norwegian-American antiques is maintained in the various buildings of the town.

The chapel at Little Norway.

The Blue Mounds region is also the location of the Cave of the Mounds. This large cavern with eighteen rooms of uniquely colored limestone formations was discovered in 1939.

Only about 19 miles (about 29 kilometers) to the south is another village with European-style buildings. This is New Glarus, which has been called "Swissconsin" because of its Swiss background. At New Glarus are the Swiss Museum Village and the Chalet of the Golden Fleece, both with many interesting old-world exhibits.

The population of New Glarus is still largely of Swiss descent, and each year many events take place to remind the visitor of Switzerland. There is the Volksfest of the Swiss Men's Chorus in August. The William Tell festival has been held on Labor Day since 1938. Its principal attraction is the pageant of "William Tell" by Schiller.

New Glarus is noted for its bell ringers, yodelers, flag throwers, and Alpine horn blowers. Many people visit its Swiss lace factory.

Nearby Monroe is known as the Swiss cheese center of America. At Spring Green, Frank Lloyd Wright's home and school, Taliesin, and his grave are much-visited sites.

To the south and west of Spring Green is Mineral Point, with its memories of rip-roaring mining days. At Mineral Point, Pendarvis offers the visitor a restoration of three authentic homes built by the miners from the nearby stone quarries. These houses are on Shakerag Street, which took its picturesque and famous name from the habit the miners' cooks had of shaking a rag on a pole as a signal for dinner.

Present-day visitors can sample a Cornish dinner at Pendarvis House. There the diners can enjoy hearty meat pie, called Cornish pasty, saffron cake, or wild plum tart with scalded cream.

Tourists in south central Wisconsin concentrate their activities in the Wisconsin Dells region. The boat trips through world-famous rock formations of the Dells are among the best known in the country. The Dells area is one of the most thoroughly organized tourist regions anywhere and offers a wide variety of interesting commercial attractions as well as scenery.

At nearby Baraboo can be found one of the truly unusual museums. The Circus World Museum helps to recall the days when

80

The William Tell festival in New Glarus.

Wisconsin was the leading circus state—when over one hundred circuses had their headquarters in the state.

One of Wisconsin's circus leaders was W. C. Coup of Delavan. Mr. Coup invented the three-ring circus and originated the idea of using special railroad cars to carry his show from place to place. His nickname, Popcorn George, came from his first job, that of selling popcorn in a circus. He was the first American to take a circus abroad by boat.

The most famous of Wisconsin's circus men were the five Ringling Brothers of Baraboo. The circus was in their blood almost from their first steps. At the first show they gave as boys, Al broke most of his mother's plates doing a juggling act, and their menagerie consisted of chickens, rabbits, a billy goat, and a horse named Zachary that they had bought from a war veteran for $8.42.

In 1882, the Ringling boys collected fifty dollars and started out from Baraboo with their first circus. Johnny Ringling, only fourteen at that time, helped arrange for the lots where the circus could be shown. One owner finally agreed to let the boys use his lot if they promised to keep the trees from harm. He was quite surprised when young Johnny pulled out a contract for him to sign.

He was even more surprised when the equipment arrived and he found that the boys had a real circus with tents and pennants and all the rest. He found the trees carefully roped off, and although his fence had been taken down to let the wagons go through it was carefully replaced when the circus was over.

Even though they were very young it was clear that the Ringling brothers were not only circus men but also businessmen. Their circus grew until it became "The Greatest Show on Earth," with headquarters in Baraboo until 1918.

Visitors at the Circus World Museum can see objects recalling the Ringlings and other circus greats of Wisconsin. The exhibits include the "world's largest miniature circus," a steam calliope, and many colorful wagons and railroad cars of the great circus days, along with a live menagerie.

The western border of Wisconsin, of course, is dominated by the great Mississippi River.

On the Mississippi in southern Wisconsin is historic Prairie du Chien, second-oldest town in the state. It has one of the most unusual names in geography. Its name in French means Prairie of the Dog. The early French named it for the Indian Chief Alim whose name means "dog" in the Indian language.

The visitor to "Dog Prairie" today will see little to remind him of the colorful life that made the town a leading fur-trading post. No longer do the blanketed and painted Indians mingle with frontiersmen in buckskin or boatmen wearing gaudy plaid shirts and earrings.

But one trace of the past remains today almost as it was in the bustling days when Prairie du Chien was second city of the state. That is the Villa Louis. This unbelievable mansion was built in 1843 by Hercules Dousman, leading fur dealer of the region who is supposed to have been Wisconsin's first millionaire. The villa became the social center of the entire northwest.

On the Dousman's private racetrack, purebred horses raced on a surface of cork imported from England. Their guests fished in stocked ponds and played pool on an elaborate table inlaid in ivory. They listened to Madame Dousman play on one of the first pianos ever brought to the Midwest.

Villa Louis has been restored as it was during the height of its grandeur. Visitors may see French "casket" bathtubs, carved rosewood furniture, Audubon plates, and a private chapel with white prayer benches. On the grounds outside the villa are a dairy, an

Villa Louis

icehouse, a preserve room, a laundry, and a school room, as well as the office where Colonel Dousman carried on his fur business as the representative of John Jacob Astor. The Old Coach House is now a museum of early community history.

The Villa Louis is thought to be the finest example of this kind of building in the United States.

Another unusual museum at Prairie du Chien is the Museum of Medical Progress. This occupies the carefully reconstructed military hospital building of the second Fort Crawford, built in 1829. The museum exhibits tell the story of the progress of medicine in the Midwest, and particularly in Wisconsin, beginning in the days of Indian medicine men who used healing rites and herbs.

South of Prairie du Chien, near Cassville, is Nelson Dewey State Park. This is the location of Stonefield Village, a replica of a crossroad village of the 1890s. The State Farm and Craft Museum here has a display of historic agricultural machinery and early handcrafts.

To the north of Prairie du Chien is another historic Mississippi River town, La Crosse. It also took its name from the Indians, by way of the French. Early Frenchmen in the region found that the present location of La Crosse was the favorite field for the Indians to play the game of lacrosse. Sometimes as many as three hundred Indians would play at one time in the rather informal and rough games on the prairie de la crosse. And so when a town sprang up there, it took the name of the Indian's favorite game, La Crosse.

Much farther north the beautiful St. Croix River becomes the western boundary of Wisconsin. On this river is Interstate State Park, near St. Croix Falls. The states of Minnesota and Wisconsin worked together to establish the park, and it is the first state park ever to be established by two states. It is also the first of Wisconsin's state parks.

In the northwest corner of the state is Pattison State Park. Manitou Falls, at Pattison Park, is the highest in the state.

Northern Wisconsin is often called a Vacation Wonderland.

The town of Rhinelander is referred to as the "Gateway to the world's most concentrated lake region." There are 232 lakes within a

The mouth of the St. Croix, painted by Henry Lewis.

short distance of the town — also eleven trout streams and two rivers. The Logging Museum at Rhinelander has one of the most complete displays of old-time lumbering. The museum houses the "Hodag," a mythical monster that was actually a noted hoax.

The Eagle River chain of twenty-seven lakes is considered to be the largest of this type of freshwater lake chain in the world.

In Ashland, on Lake Superior, was the first house built by a white settler in what is now Wisconsin. The location is marked by a stone monument. The waters of Chequamegon Bay at Ashland are said to be the "Shining Big Sea Water" mentioned in Longfellow's *Hiawatha.*

At Ashland's harbor in Chequamegon Bay, ships dock to load millions of tons of ore brought from the Gogebic Range in Michigan. The city takes its name from Henry Clay's famous estate in Kentucky.

North of Ashland, forming the northernmost part of the state, are the Apostle Islands, that can be reached from the town of Bayfield.

Although there were only twelve Apostles, there are twenty-three Apostle Islands. Largest of these is Madeline. On Madeline Island an unusual craft shop is operated by one of the local churches for the benefit of the church. Crafts sold in this shop are made on the island itself.

At the very western tip of Lake Superior is the great seaport shared by Wisconsin's Superior and Minnesota's Duluth. This is called the westernmost of the great inland seaports. The docks are the largest in the country. One of the ten huge grain elevators is the tallest in the world. Superior also has a shipyard, flour mill, two briquet plants, and seven coal docks.

Although vacationing was once possible only in the summer, now popular winter sports make the state attractive as a vacation area all year. Some of the fastest iceboats race across the frozen lakes. Where the ice fishing is good, the frozen surfaces of the lakes are so crowded with ice fishing shacks that they sometimes look like small cities. Skiing, skating, and other winter sports are both popular and abundant in the "Land Where the Waters Gather," where the motto is "Forward."

Dutch Festival in Cedar Grove

Handy Reference Section

Became 30th state—May 29, 1848
Capital—Madison
State bird—Robin
State flower—Wood Violet
State tree—Sugar Maple
State stone—Red Granite
State mineral—Galena (lead)
State song—"On Wisconsin"
State animal—Badger
State wildlife animal—White-Tailed Deer
State fish—Muskellunge
State motto—*Forward*
Area—65,154 square miles (145,438 square kilometers)
Rank in size—26th
Greatest length (north to south—320 miles (515 kilometers)
Greatest width (east to west—295 miles (475 kilometers)
Highest point—Timms Hill, Prince County, 1,952 feet (595 meters)
Lowest point—581 feet (177 meters)
Highest recorded temperature—114°F (46°C)
Lowest recorded temperature—minus 54°F (-48°C)
Population—4,985,000 (1978 est.)
Rank in nation—16th
Population Density—79 persons per square mile, 1974 est.
                (31 persons per square kilometer)
Birthrate—14.2 per 1000
Physicians—124 per 100,000

Principal cities—		
Milwaukee	774,761	(1978 est.)
Madison	185,767	
Racine	102,774	
Green Bay	94,833	
Kenosha	85,109	
Appleton	61,714	
Oshkosh	57,488	

You Have A Date with History

1634 Jean Nicolet, first white men in Wisconsin
1654-1656 Radisson and Groseilliers, first fur traders
1661 Father Réne Ménard, first missionary to Wisconsin Indians
1673 Jolliet and Marquette discover upper Mississippi
1678 Duluth explores western ene of Lake Superior
1763 Treaty of Paris, Wisconsin becomes English territory
1764 Langlade settles at Green Bay, first permanent settlement
1783 Treaty of Paris, Wisconsin becomes part of new America
1815 War with England is over
1818 Solomon Juneau at Milwaukee
1832 Black Hawk War
1835 First steamboat arrived at Milwaukee
1836 Act creating Territory of Wisconsin signed
1848 Wisconsin becomes state
1851 First railroad train, Milwaukee to Waukesha
1854 Republican Party formed at Ripon
1859 Abraham Lincoln spoke at State Fair in Milwaukee
1861 Beginning of Civil War
1865 Civil War closes
1869 Typewriter invented by Sholes
1871 Destructive forest fires
1890 Babcock milk test discovered
1901 Robert M. La Follette becomes governor
1904 Primary election law approved
1905 State civil service established
1908 Income tax amendment adopted
1917 First World War; state Capitol completed
1929 Prof. Steenbock patents radiation of Vitamin D.
1932 United States Forest Products Laboratory established
1941 World War II
1948 Centennial year
1957 Milwaukee Braves win pennant and world championship
1960 Mrs. Dena Smith, state treasurer, first woman elected
to state office in Wisconsin
1961 Menominee becomes seventy-second county of Wisconsin
1975 Menominee seize Alexian Brothers Estate
1977 Governor Patrick Lucey appointed U. S. Ambassador to Mexico

Thinkers, Doers, Fighters

Men and Women Who Helped Make Wisconsin Great

Stephen Babcock
Carrie Jacobs Bond
Hamlin Garland
William Hoard
Robert M. La Follette
Charles Langlade
Increase Allen Lapham
William ''Billy'' Mitchell
Vinnie Ream
Christopher L. Sholes
John Stevens
Harry Steenbock
Frederick Jackson Turner
Charles R. Van Hise
Tomah, Chief of the Menominees
Frank Lloyd Wright

Annual Events
May—Cherry Blossom Time, Door County
June—Sparta Dairy Days, Sparta
July—Musky Jamboree, Boulder Junction
July and August—Indian Pow-Wows, Lac Du Flambeau
August—Swiss Volksfest, New Glarus
August—Bratwurst Day, Sheboygan
August—Wisconsin State Fair, Milwaukee
August—Menominee Indian Pageant, Shawano
September—Road America Sports Car Competition, Elkhart Lake
September—William Tell Anniversary, New Glarus
November—Holiday Folk Fair, Milwaukee

Governors of Wisconsin

Nelson Dewey 1848-1852
Leonard J. Farwell 1852-1854
William Augustus Barstow 1854-1856
Arthur MacArthur 1856
Coles Bashford 1856-1858
Alexander W. Randall 1858-1862
Louis P. Harvey 1862
Edward Salomon 1862-1864
James T. Lewis 1864-1866
Lucius Fairchild 1866-1872
Cadwallader C. Washburn 1872-1874
William R. Taylor 1874-1876
Harrison Ludington 1876-1878
William E. Smith 1878-1882
Jeremiah McLain Rusk 1882-1889
William D. Hoard 1889-1891
George W. Peck 1891-1895
William H. Upham 1895-1897
Edward Scofield 1897-1901
Robert M. LaFollette 1901-1906
James O. Davidson 1906-1922

Francis E. McGovern 1911-1915
Emanuel L. Philipp 1915-1921
John J. Blaine 1921-1927
Fred R. Zimmerman 1927-1929
Walter J. Kohler 1929-1931
Philip F. LaFollette 1931-1933
Albert G. Schmedeman 1933-1935
Philip F. LaFollette 1935-1939
Julius P. Heil 1939-1943
Orland S. Loomis Died before
   inaugurated
Walter S. Goodland 1943-1947
Oscar Rennebohm 1947-1951
Walter J. Kohler, Jr. 1951-1957
Vernon W. Thomson 1957-1959
Gaylord A. Nelson 1959-1963
John W. Reynolds 1963-1965
Warren P. Knowles 1965-1971
Patrick Lucey 1975-1977
Martin J. Schreiber sworn in
   July 7,1977

Index

91

PICTURE CREDITS

ABOUT THE AUTHOR

With the publication of his first book for school use when he was twenty, **Allan Carpenter** began a career as an author that has spanned more than 135 books. After teaching in the public schools of Des Moines, Mr. Carpenter began his career as an educational publisher at the age of twenty-one when he founded the magazine *Teachers Digest.* In the field of educational periodicals, he was responsible for many innovations. During his many years in publishing, he has perfected a highly organized approach to handling large volumes of factual material: after extensive traveling and having collected all possible materials, he systematically reviews and organizes everything. From his apartment high in Chicago's John Hancock Building, Allan recalls, "My collection and assimilation of materials on the states and countries began before the publication of my first book." Allan is the founder of Carpenter Publishing House and of Infordata International, Inc., publishers of *Issues in Education* and *Index to U. S. Government Periodicals.* When he is not writing or traveling, his principal avocation is music. He has been the principal bassist of many symphonies, and he managed the country's leading non-professional symphony for twenty-five years.